The Purpose of Prayer

⑂ Precept®

ISBN: 978-1-6368-721-62

Copyright © 2024 by Precept®. All rights reserved.

This material is published by and is the sole property of Precept of Chattanooga, Tennessee. No part of this publication may be reproduced, translated, or transmitted in any form or by any means, electronic or mechanical, including photocopying, recording, or any information storage and retrieval system, without permission in writing from the publisher.

Precept, Precept Ministries International, Precept Ministries International The Inductive Bible Study People, the Plumb Bob design, Precept Upon Precept, In & Out, Sweeter than Chocolate!, Cookies on the Lower Shelf, Precepts For Life, Precepts From God's Word, Transform Student Ministries, and Know God Deeply Studies are trademarks of Precept.

Unless otherwise noted, all Scripture taken from ESV Bible (The Holy Bible, English Standard Version®). Copyright © 2001, 2007, 2011, 2016 by Crossway Books and Bibles, a Publishing Ministry of Good News Publishers. Used by permission. All rights reserved.

First Edition. August 2024

Created in Chattanooga, TN

Know God Deeply™ Studies

The Purpose of Prayer

A Collection on Prayer, Volume One

Precept®

THE **PURPOSE** OF PRAYER

CONTENTS //

WEEK 1

6 // **Lesson One:** *Introduction*

15 // **Opening Group Discussion Questions**

17 // **Lesson Two:** *I Am the Vine; You Are the Branches*
John 15

23 // **Lesson Three:** *Abide in Me*
John 15

29 // **Lesson Four:** *Whatever You Ask*
John 15

35 // **Lesson Five:** *Prayer at a Glance*
John 15

37 // **Week One:** *Group Discussion Questions*

WEEK 2

42 // **Lesson Six:** *Dwelling and Abiding*
Psalm 91

47 // **Lesson Seven:** *When You Pray*
Matthew 6

55 // **Lesson Eight:** *Our Father*
Matthew 6

63 // **Lesson Nine:** *The Father Knows*
Matthew 6

69 // **Lesson Ten:** *Prayer at a Glance*
Psalm 91; Matthew 6

71 // **Week Two:** *Group Discussion Questions*

WEEK 3

76 // **Lesson Eleven:** *My Father*
Matthew 26

83 // **Lesson Twelve:** *A Sorrowful Soul*
Matthew 26

89 // **Lesson Thirteen:** *As You Will*
Matthew 26

95 // **Lesson Fourteen:** *Winning the Battle through Prayer*
Matthew 26

101 // **Lesson Fifteen:** *Prayer at a Glance*
Matthew 26

A Collection on Prayer, Volume One

103 // **Week Three:** *Group Discussion Questions*

WEEK 4

108 // **Lesson Sixteen:** *History with God*
Daniel 1

115 // **Lesson Seventeen:** *God Comes Through*
Daniel 2

121 // **Lesson Eighteen:** *But If Not . . .*
Daniel 3

127 // **Lesson Nineteen:** *Draw Near*
James 4

133 // **Lesson Twenty:** *Prayer at a Glance*
Daniel 1–3; James 4

135 // **Week Four:** *Group Discussion Questions*

CONCLUSION

141 // **Closing Group Discussion Questions**

APPENDIX

143 // **Scripture Observation Sheets**
John 15
Psalm 91
Matthew 6
Matthew 26
Daniel 1–3
James 4

161 // **Prayer at a Glance**

WEEK 1

Lesson One: Introduction //

It is no secret that relationships take work. They need time, intentionality, and effort. They must be cultivated and nurtured. Relationships require constant humility and forgiveness. But at their best, they are worth it.

The same is true for our relationship with God. We are invited into deep intimacy with the Father because of all Jesus has done for us. Through His teaching and example, Jesus showed us a way to foster this nearness with the Father—prayer.

But even for lifelong Christians, prayer can become elusive, boring, or obligatory—and sometimes, all three. We believe we *should* pray. We may even *want* to pray. But we become lost in the *how* and *why* of it.

The goal of this Collection on Prayer is to return to the basics and explore all aspects of prayer. *What* is prayer? *Why* do we pray? And *How?* In this first volume, we will get to the heart of the matter—the purpose of prayer. Together we will turn to Scripture to uncover the reason we pray.

As you study, our prayer is that you will encounter the heart of the Father, grow in a loving relationship with Him, and find ways to commune with Him each day.

THE METHOD

We believe that relationship with God comes through knowing His Word. Studying the Bible allows us to know God deeply and live differently, being transformed into the image of Jesus.

We approach Bible study with a hands-on method. The Bible is thousands of years old, and it becomes easy to skim over strange stories or familiar verses without true understanding. To help you explore Scripture for yourself, we rely on the Precept Bible Study Method:

- **Observe:** What does the text say?
- **Interpret:** What does the text mean?
- **Apply:** How should the meaning affect my life?

Taken together, these three components help you slow down, discover meaning, and find connections to your daily life.

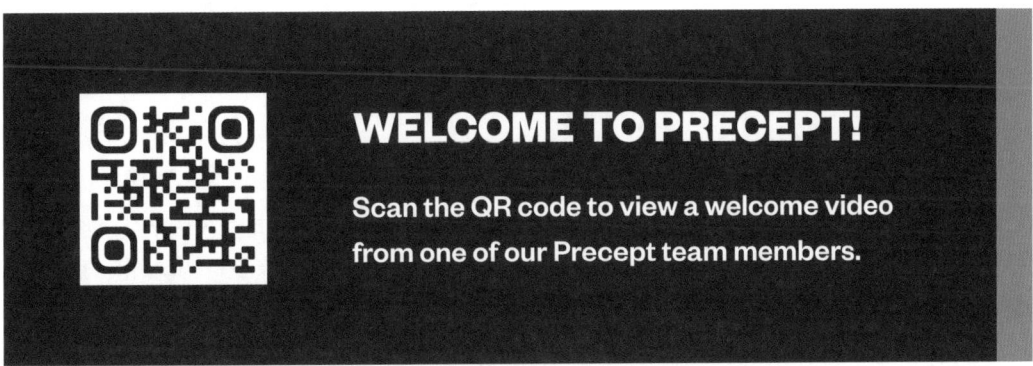

precept.org/essentials

THE METHOD //

OBSERVE

The purpose of observation is to understand what the text says. As you seek to observe Scripture carefully and accurately, the following tools will help.

Begin with Prayer
The Bible study process begins with prayer. Although prayer is often a missing or overlooked element, its importance cannot be overemphasized. No matter how good our method or tools, true understanding and life change only come through God.

Answer the 5Ws and an H
You will answer straightforward questions like *who, what, when, where, why,* and *how* using a particular passage of text. These questions are the building blocks for detailed observation. Answering these questions will allow you to read *on purpose,* for the goal of understanding. This exercise will help you note the details of what you are reading so you won't miss anything. No special knowledge or insight is required.

Mark Key Words and Phrases
A key word is one that is essential to the text. Key words and phrases are repeated to convey the author's point or purpose for writing. To mark a key word or phrase, you will

visually distinguish it with a symbol, color, or combination of the two. Once marked, you will see at a glance where and how often the word or phrase appears. This step may also include making notes on comparisons, contrasts, or terms of conclusion. Marking may seem arbitrary in the moment, but it will help you pick up on themes and important points the author wants you to catch.

Make Lists

Making lists is to record all the details about something or someone in one place. Then you can review and reflect on everything you discover about a topic. This is most helpful when there is a lot of information scattered across several verses or chapters (for example, the miracles of Jesus or the story of creation).

Identify Chapter Themes

The theme of a chapter will center on the main person, event, teaching, or subject of that section of Scripture. Themes are often revealed by reviewing the key words and lists you developed.

THE METHOD

Scan the QR code to learn more about our Bible Study Method.

∴ INTERPRET

While observation leads to an accurate understanding of what the Word of God says, interpretation goes a step further to help you understand what it means. Thorough and careful observation flows into accurate interpretation. As you seek to interpret the Bible accurately, the following tools will be helpful.

Context
Scripture is a beautiful tapestry. When we observe a text, we focus on a small piece of the larger tapestry. We must also pay attention to the weave binding the material together. The context weaves throughout the entire biblical tapestry and binds it together. To discover the context, we will pay attention to the historical and cultural context, the surrounding verses, the theme and structure of the entire book, other passages across the Bible on the same topic, and the overall story of redemption in Scripture. It is important that we never take Scripture out of its context to make it say what we want it to say. Keeping context in mind enables us to discover what the author is saying rather than adding to their meaning.

Cross-References
Cross-references identify commonalities throughout different parts of Scripture. They allow us to trace the thread of common themes, words, events, or people. Studying cross-references helps us to seek the full counsel of the Word of God.

Word Studies
Our English Bibles vary from one translation to another. Different versions may use varying English words or phrases to translate a single Greek or Hebrew word. The tool of word studies helps us to accurately explore the meaning of a text by looking at the original Greek or Hebrew word behind the English word we are studying.

Sometimes interpretation is straightforward with an obvious answer. Other times, it's more nuanced. The Bible requires lifelong study, and the more you explore and meditate on Scripture, the more your understanding will grow day by day.

APPLY

Once you have seen what a text says and understood what it means, you can begin to consider how it affects your daily life. There are two primary ways we can apply the Scripture we read.

The first is a change of belief. Sometimes what you read will apply to matters of the heart or mind (and often, both). In this case, application takes us from simply knowing random facts to truly believing and living in light of that belief. Secondly, application leads to a change of behavior. Sometimes a text applies directly to something you can do or change externally in your life.

We will guide you through application with questions like:

What would change in your life if _____ were true?
What would be different in my life if I lived like God was _____?
How is your perspective on [current issue] affected by what you just read?
What steps can you take this week to _____?

Without application, Bible study is little more than an interesting academic exercise. This is where it is most important to involve others. Christians need other Christians, and you will find that your experience is richer and more enjoyable if you involve community in what you are learning.

A group discussion guide follows each week of study. We invite you to study alongside a group to help you reason through the Scriptures as you share ideas, discoveries, and prayers within your group.

And most importantly, it is essential that we involve the Spirit. Through Jesus and the power of the Holy Spirit, true belief and real-life change begin to take place.

THE **PURPOSE** OF PRAYER

PAUSE AND REFLECT

Before we begin Bible study, let's start by reflecting on some of your current thoughts and practices regarding prayer. Take some time to consider the questions below and write out your thoughts in the space provided or in your own journal. If you have other questions or hopes as you begin this study, reflect on those as well and express them to God.

1 // How do you pray? What do your prayer rhythms and routines currently look like? *If you don't currently have these rhythms and routines in place, don't worry! We will help you develop some throughout this study.*

2 // Why do you pray?

3 // Think of the most important relationship in your life. Perhaps it is a family member, a best friend, or a spouse. What makes this relationship so special? How do you nurture it so that it grows and thrives? Why do you nurture it? How is this similar or different to how you treat your relationship with God?

4 // What are some obstacles or challenges to prayer in your life?

PRAY

One of the most important things about prayer is consistency—simply showing up. We will give you opportunities at the end of each lesson to turn to the Father in prayer. Today we have a guided prayer for you. Read through the words slowly, using them to guide your conversation with God.

Father God,

*You are the God of the universe,
the Creator of it all.
You are great, magnificent, and powerful.*

And yet . . .

*You see me. You know me. You love me.
And You want to be in communion with me.
May I always remember this.*

*As we begin this journey through Your Word,
May the truth that You desire an intimate relationship with me
continue to draw me back to You and Your heart,
each and every day.*

*Lord, I echo David's prayer to You,
Show me Your ways, my God.
Teach me Your path.
Lead me in Your truth and teach me.*

*I love You.
I can't wait to know You and love You even more.*

Amen.

OPENING GROUP DISCUSSION QUESTIONS

We have seen that genuine transformation and growth often involve other people. We encourage you to study alongside a group of believers. This study provides discussion questions along the way. As you begin your group this week, discuss your answers and reflections from the "Pause and Reflect" section on page 13 of your study.

Opening Questions: What are your hopes as you begin this study? What questions do you have for God regarding prayer?

1 // How do you pray? What do your rhythms and routines of prayer currently look like?

2 // Why do you pray?

3 // Think of the most important relationship in your life. Perhaps it is a family member, a best friend, or a spouse. What makes this relationship so special? How do you nurture it so that it grows and thrives? Why do you nurture it? How is this similar or different to how you treat your relationship with God?

4 // What are some obstacles or challenges to prayer in your life?

Closing: End your time together by asking each member of your group to share their personal prayer requests. Then, spend time praying for one another. Commit to praying for each other throughout the week.

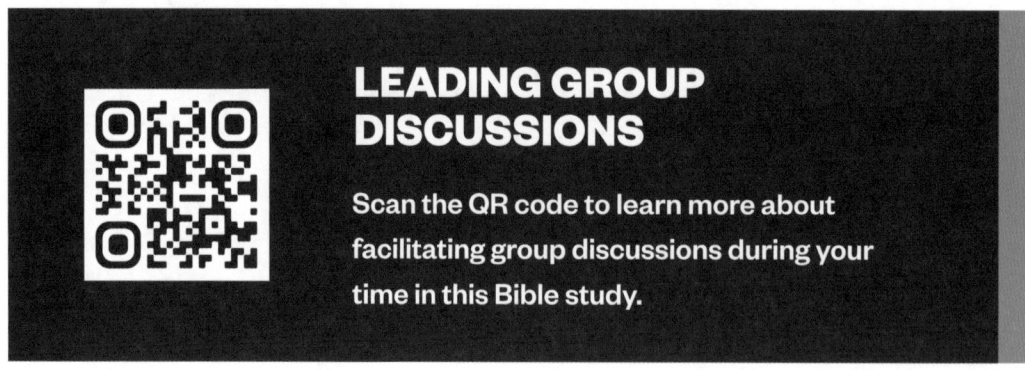

LEADING GROUP DISCUSSIONS

Scan the QR code to learn more about facilitating group discussions during your time in this Bible study.

A Collection on Prayer, Volume One

THE PURPOSE OF PRAYER

Lesson Two:
I Am the Vine;
You Are the Branches

JOHN 15

Prayer begins with relationship. We will explore the purpose of prayer in the Gospel of John. In this passage, Jesus speaks some powerful words about being in relationship with Him and His Father. We will build our understanding of why we pray on this foundation.

Read John 15:1–17.

In the Appendix, you will find an Observation Sheet with the text of John 15.

As you read, mark each of the following:

1 // references to *the Father* (including pronouns such as *he, him,* and *his*) with a purple triangle

2 // references to Jesus (including pronouns such as *I, me,* and *my*) with a red cross

3 // the word *fruit* with an orange box

It may help to read through the passage multiple times, marking each reference or word one at a time. Or, if you prefer, you can mark them all during a single read-through. Do what works best for you.

⋯ Let's observe what Jesus teaches.

1 // Jesus uses an analogy in this passage. What does He compare Himself to? His Father? Each of us?

2 // Based on this analogy, what is the nature of the relationship between each of these?

3 // How do the branches bear fruit?

4 // Make a list of everything that happens when we bear fruit.

5 // What do we learn about Jesus' relationship with His Father?

6 // Why does Jesus tell us that He has spoken these things?

THE PURPOSE OF PRAYER

In the next chapter, Jesus goes on to tell us how we can access this full joy! Read John 16:23–24.

As you read, mark each of the following:

1 // the word *joy* with a circle

2 // the word *ask* with a blue arrow pointing up

> **John 16**
> 23 In that day you will ask nothing of me. Truly, truly, I say to you, whatever you ask of the Father in my name, he will give it to you.
> 24 Until now you have asked nothing in my name. Ask, and you will receive, that your joy may be full.

7 // How will our joy be made full?

8 // What do Jesus' words teach us about prayer? And how are we to ask and receive?

Reflect and Apply.

9 // What do Jesus' words in John 15–16 show us about His desires for us and our relationship with Him?

10 // How would you describe your current relationship with Jesus? How is it similar or different to the relationship Jesus is describing here?

11 // How has your relationship and prayer life with Jesus brought you joy?

12 // Relationships take work and intentionality. What are some practical ways you can grow in your relationship with Jesus this week?

THE PURPOSE OF PRAYER

PRAY

A wonderful first step to growing in your relationship with Christ is to spend some time with Him today. Sit with Him like you are sitting with a friend. Picture yourself with Him in the room. Tell Him about your day and anything that is on your mind. Or simply be still and quiet before Him. If it is helpful for you to write out your prayer to Him, you can do so in the space provided.

A Collection on Prayer, Volume One

THE PURPOSE OF PRAYER

Lesson Three: Abide in Me //

JOHN 15

Jesus desires to be in relationship with us. And it is prayer that helps us to nurture this relationship and abide in Him. Let's jump back into John 15 to discover more.

Read John 15:1–17 again.

This time, mark the word *abide* with a green circle.

Let's take a closer look.

1 // Make a list of everything you learn from the word *abide*.

2 // Looking at your list, what is Jesus asking us to abide in?

3 // What does it mean to abide in Jesus and His love? Why is this important?

4 // Let's take a closer look at the meaning of the word *abide*. Take some time to look up the Greek word. Write the transliteration, definition, and anything else you learn about the word.

WORD STUDIES

Scan the QR code for a step-by-step guide on how to do a word study.

THE PURPOSE OF PRAYER

To help us understand Jesus' teaching, let's take a look at where God dwelt with His people in the Old Testament. Read Exodus 40:34–38.

As you read, mark the word *tabernacle* (including the pronoun *it*) with a circle.

> **Exodus 40**
> 34 Then the cloud covered the tent of meeting, and the glory of the Lord filled the tabernacle.
> 35 And Moses was not able to enter the tent of meeting because the cloud settled on it, and the glory of the Lord filled the tabernacle.
> 36 Throughout all their journeys, whenever the cloud was taken up from over the tabernacle, the people of Israel would set out.
> 37 But if the cloud was not taken up, then they did not set out till the day that it was taken up.
> 38 For the cloud of the Lord was on the tabernacle by day, and fire was in it by night, in the sight of all the house of Israel throughout all their journeys.

5 // Where did God dwell with His people?

6 // How did God's glory manifest itself both in and outside the tabernacle? How did it guide the Israelites?

7 // Look up the Hebrew word for *tabernacle*. Write the transliteration, definition, and anything else you learn about the word. How is this word similar to the Greek word for *abide*?

8 // This passage of Scripture occurred during Moses and the Israelites' wandering in the wilderness. With this in mind, how might God's presence and guidance have impacted them on their journey?

9 // God once dwelt with His people in a tabernacle. Where does He abide now?

10 // How do you experience the reality of Jesus' abiding and dwelling in you? How does this reality affect your day-to-day life?

11 // Jesus calls us to abide in Him as He abides in us. We are all abiding, or making our home, in *something*. Our "abiding place" could be the place our mind returns to when it is at rest, where we spend most of our time and energy, and where we spend our money. When you reflect on this, where do you find yourself most often abiding?

THE PURPOSE OF PRAYER

12 // What would it look like for you to abide most often in Jesus? How would doing so affect your daily life?
Take your time answering this, bringing it up to Jesus in prayer. Be as specific as you can.

PRAY

Simply abide in Jesus today and ask Him for the grace to recognize that He is abiding in you. Sit and rest in this love exchange. Carry this awareness with you throughout your day. Return to Him often and take notice of how your abiding transforms your thoughts, words, and actions as you go about your day. Return to this page at the end of your day or tomorrow to record your thoughts on how your day went while consciously abiding in Jesus.

THE PURPOSE OF PRAYER

Lesson Four: Whatever You Ask

JOHN 15

We have spent the past few days unpacking John 15, exploring the relationship between Jesus and the Father and, in turn, our relationship with our Heavenly Father. Now let's take a look at what Jesus teaches about how to approach our Father in prayer.

Read John 15:1–17 once more.

This time, mark the word *ask* with a blue arrow pointing up.

1 // What is Jesus' promise to us in verse 7?

2 // Jesus qualifies this promise with the word *if.* What is He asking of us?

3 // Let's look at verse 16. What is Jesus asking of us here?

4 // Mark the phrase *so that* with an arrow pointing to the right. Why does Jesus ask this of us?

5 // What connection does Jesus make between abiding in Him and prayer?

6 // How does your relationship with God influence your prayer life? And vice versa, how does your prayer life affect your relationship with God?

THE PURPOSE OF PRAYER

Read Psalm 37:4.

As you read, mark references to the *Lord* with a purple triangle.

> **Psalm 37**
> 4 Delight yourself in the LORD,
>   and he will give you the desires of your heart.

7 // What does King David invite us to do in these verses?

8 // What will be the result of this action?

9 // What does it look like for you to delight in the Lord? How does doing so affect your heart and mind, your thoughts and emotions?

10 // How might delighting in the Lord begin to transform the desires of your heart? Similarly, how might abiding in Jesus begin to transform the things we ask and pray for?

11 // As we delight in the Lord and abide in Him, growing in our relationship with Him, our hearts and desires begin to align with His good desires for us. How have you experienced this in your relationship with the Lord?

12 // Reflect on your prayers. How do you see yourself praying in alignment with God's desires for you? How can you continue to work toward praying this way?

THE PURPOSE OF PRAYER

PRAY

Give thanks to God for the gift of being in a relationship with Him. Bring to Him anything that is in your heart, including any questions that may have been stirred up. Bring your heart to Him, authentically and honestly, trusting in His great love for you.

Lesson Five: Prayer at a Glance

In the Appendix, we have provided a *Prayer at a Glance* chart. Pause and reflect on what God taught you through your time in His Word. We encourage you to take your time filling it out, going back to reread John 15 and reviewing your answers if necessary. Fill in as much of the chart as you can. We will return to it throughout the study, and by the end, you will have gathered a full picture of the purpose of prayer from Scripture.

Pray without Ceasing

In 1 Thessalonians 5:16–18, Paul instructs us to:

> **1 Thessalonians 5**
> 16 Rejoice always,
> 17 pray without ceasing,
> 18 give thanks in all circumstances, for this is the will of God in Christ Jesus for you.

We will give you opportunities to put these words into practice throughout this study. It is easy for prayer to become a small part of our day. But what if we took Paul at his word and truly prayed without ceasing, rejoicing in the Lord and thanking Him throughout our day?

When you think about the significant relationships in your life, how do you stay connected to them? Sometimes it may be through a short text or sharing a video that reminds you of them. Other times, it is long conversations and hours of quality time.

Our time with God is like this. Sometimes we may set aside intentional time to pray with Him. At other times, we can simply invite Him into our lives by lifting up our hearts and minds to Him in the midst of our daily responsibilities and busy schedules.

Practice praying without ceasing today by abiding in Christ and letting His words abide in you. Write out some truths from John 15 that you would like to carry with you as you go about your day. You can write these on a notecard you keep in your wallet or a sticky note for your desk. Pause often to think of Jesus and the truth of His words, letting them lead you deeper into prayer.

THE PURPOSE OF PRAYER

WEEK ONE: GROUP DISCUSSION QUESTIONS

Opening Question: How would you explain prayer to someone who has never experienced it?

1 // Observe (Lesson 2, questions 1 and 2, page 18): Jesus uses an analogy throughout John 15. What does He compare Himself to? His Father? Each of us? What is the nature of the relationship between each of these?

Apply (Lesson 2, question 10, page 20): How would you describe your current relationship with Jesus? How is it similar or different to the relationship Jesus describes in John 15?

2 // Interpret (Lesson 3, question 3, page 24): Based on your reading of John 15, what does it mean to abide in Jesus and His love? Why is this important?

Apply (Lesson 3, questions 11 and 12, pages 26 and 27): Where do you find yourself most commonly abiding? What would it look like for you to abide most often in Jesus? How would doing so affect your daily life?

3 // Interpret (Lesson 4, question 5, page 30): What connection does Jesus make between abiding in Him and prayer?

Apply (Lesson 4, question 6, page 30): How does your relationship with God influence your prayer life? And vice versa, how does your prayer life affect your relationship with God?

Apply (Lesson 4, question 12, page 32): When you think about your prayers, how do you see yourself praying in alignment with God's desires for you? How can you continue to work toward praying this way?

A Collection on Prayer, Volume One

4 // Prayer at a Glance (Lesson 5, page 35): What did God teach you during your time in John 15? What were your personal takeaways? How have the truths of John 15 begun to impact your life?

Closing: End your time together by asking each member of your group to share their personal prayer requests. Then, spend time praying for one another. Commit to praying for each other throughout the week.

WEEK 1 WRAP-UP

Scan the QR code to listen to a roundtable discussion on what we have explored about prayer in John 15.

WEEK 2

Lesson Six: Dwelling and Abiding

PSALM 91

Last week we dug into Jesus' words in John 15 and His call to abide in Him. As we begin our second week of study, let's explore a psalm that echoes this message.

Read Psalm 91.

In the Appendix, you will find an Observation Sheet with the text of Psalm 91.

As you read, mark each of the following:

1 // references to *God* (including names such as *Most High* and *Almighty* and pronouns such as *he* and *I*) with a purple triangle

2 // references to the psalmist or his audience (including pronouns such as *he, I, my,* and *you*) with an orange box

3 // the words *dwell* and *abide* with a green circle

4 // the word *refuge* with a blue underline

It may help to read through the passage multiple times, marking each reference or word one at a time. Or, if you prefer, you can mark them all during a single read-through. Do what works best for you.

THE PURPOSE OF PRAYER

Let's take a closer look.

1 // What does the psalmist declare about who God is and what He will do? Make a list.

2 // How does the psalmist encourage us to relate to God throughout the psalm? Make a list.

3 // How would you describe the relationship between God and the person whom the psalmist is speaking about? What similarities do you see when you compare this to your relationship with God? In what areas would you like to grow in your relationship with Him?

4 // Rewrite the first verse of this psalm into your own words. What do these words mean to you?

5 // What other places do you find yourself running to from time to time—instead of the "shelter of the Most High" and "shadow of the Almighty"? Why do you think you turn to these places rather than God?

6 // How would it shape your life to constantly dwell and abide in God? What steps can you take to draw near to God in this way?

7 // In what ways do you see God's care and protection throughout the psalm? How have you experienced this in your life?

8 // How have these experiences led you into deeper trust and confidence in the Father as the psalmist describes?

9 // The point of view shifts in verses 14–16. Who is speaking in these final verses?

10 // List the blessings God gives in these verses.

11 // How does holding fast to God in love and knowing His name relate to the blessings He gives?

THE PURPOSE OF PRAYER

Reread John 15:7.

As you read, mark each of the following:

1 // the word *abide* with a green circle

2 // the word *ask* with a blue arrow pointing up

> **John 15**
> 7   If you abide in me, and my words abide in you, ask whatever you wish, and it will be done for you.

12 // How do the psalmist's words and the blessings of God spoken in Psalm 91 relate to Jesus' words in John 15?

13 // How can prayer help you live out the words of this psalm—to abide and dwell, to hold fast to God in love, and to know His name? How would doing these things impact your relationship with God?

PRAY

Practice dwelling and abiding in the Father today. Sit with Him and worship Him as your refuge, fortress, and deliverer. Rest in His blessings and promises to you. Continue to do so as you go about your day, abiding in the shelter and refuge of God.

THE PURPOSE OF PRAYER

Lesson Seven: When You Pray

MATTHEW 6

In Scripture, prayer was an essential part of Jesus' life and ministry. Not only did He teach about it at great length, but He lived and modeled it for us. We will explore one of His teachings in Matthew 6 where Jesus teaches us how to pray.

Read Matthew 6:1–21.

In the Appendix, you will find an Observation Sheet with the text of Matthew 6.

As you read, mark each of the following:

1 // write Giving/Praying/Fasting in the margins where Jesus is teaching about each topic

2 // references to Jesus' audience (including pronouns such as *you* and *your*) with an orange box

3 // references to the *hypocrites* and *Gentiles* (including pronouns such as *they* and *their*) with a red circle

It may help to read through the passage multiple times, marking each reference or word one at a time. Or, if you prefer, you can mark them all during a single read-through. Do what works best for you.

Let's break down Jesus' instructions for us.

Using your markings, fill in the chart below with what the hypocrites/Gentiles are doing and what Jesus calls His followers to do. Feel free to paraphrase.

	HYPOCRITES/GENTILES	BELIEVERS
When Giving		
When Praying		
When Fasting		

THE PURPOSE OF PRAYER

1 // Contrast what Jesus says about the hypocrites and Gentiles and what He asks of His believers. What is the main difference between the two?

Read Matthew 6:1–21 once more.

This time, mark each of the following:

1 // the word *secret* with an underline

2 // the word *reward* with a double underline

2 // Where do the hypocrites and Gentiles receive their reward from?

3 // How do the believers receive their reward? Where does their reward come from?

4 // Where in your life do you sometimes struggle and act as the hypocrites and Gentiles? What earthly rewards tempt you to act in this way?

5 // Look up the Greek word for *room* in verse 6. Write the transliteration, definition, and anything else you learn about the word.

6 // What does it look like for you to go into your "inner room" and pray to the Father in secret? What is the importance of spending time alone with Him in this way?

Read Luke 18:9–14.

As you read, mark each of the following:

1 // references to the *Pharisee* with a red circle

2 // references to the *tax collector* with an orange box

> **Luke 18**
> 9 He also told this parable to some who trusted in themselves that they were righteous, and treated others with contempt:
> 10 "Two men went up into the temple to pray, one a Pharisee and the other a tax collector.
> 11 The Pharisee, standing by himself, prayed thus: 'God, I thank you that I am not like other men, extortioners, unjust, adulterers, or even like this tax collector.
> 12 I fast twice a week; I give tithes of all that I get.'
> 13 But the tax collector, standing far off, would not even lift up his eyes to heaven, but beat his breast, saying, 'God, be merciful to me, a sinner!'
> 14 I tell you, this man went down to his house justified, rather than the other. For everyone who exalts himself will be humbled, but the one who humbles himself will be exalted."

THE PURPOSE OF PRAYER

7 // To whom does Jesus tell this parable?

8 // Looking at your markings, contrast the Pharisee and tax collector. What differences does Jesus highlight between them and the way they pray?

9 // What does Jesus teach through this parable?

10 // How does this parable relate to Jesus' instructions in Matthew 6?

Look back at Matthew 6:7–8.

11 // Do you ever struggle with feeling like your prayers need to be said a certain way or your words need to be eloquent? How do Jesus' words here resist that notion? What does He want from us instead?

12 // How do these verses give you confidence when praying to your Father?

13 // Jesus tells us that the Father already knows what we need, yet He still calls us to pray and ask Him. What does this show us about the Father's heart toward us?

THE PURPOSE OF PRAYER

PRAY

Give thanks to God for being a Father who meets us in prayer. Find some time today to pray as Jesus teaches us to—go into your "inner room," shut the door, and pray to the Father in secret. Just the two of you. Humbly pour your heart out to Him, give Him praise, or just sit with Him in silence, knowing with confidence that He is with you and knows your every need.

A Collection on Prayer, Volume One

Lesson Eight: Our Father

MATTHEW 6

Not only did Jesus give His followers instructions on how to pray, but He also gave them the very words to pray. As we return to Matthew 6, we will take a closer look at the prayer Jesus taught them—the Lord's Prayer.

Read Matthew 6:9–15.

This is likely a familiar passage to you. Even so, we encourage you to read through it slowly as if for the first time.

As you read, mark each of the following:

  1 // references to the *Father* (including the pronoun *your*) with a purple triangle

  2 // references to *us* (including pronouns such as *our* and *we*) with an orange box

A Collection on Prayer, Volume One

This prayer is rich! Let's begin by looking at it as a whole.

1 // Looking at your markings, Jesus' prayer has a clear structure. What is the focus of the first half of the prayer? What is the focus of the second half?

2 // Make a list of the requests Jesus teaches us to make to God.

Now, let's take it line by line.

3 // What two words does this prayer begin with? Why is this significant?

4 // Jesus begins this prayer by hallowing God's name, which means bringing Him reverence, honor, and praise. How does beginning our prayer this way influence the heart and posture with which we approach the rest of the prayer?

5 // Verse 10 brings to God a request beyond ourselves. What is the importance of praying in alignment with God's kingdom and His will? How does this help us to prepare our hearts for the rest of the prayer?

THE PURPOSE OF PRAYER

6 // In verse 11, Jesus offers us an opportunity to present our own requests and needs to God. What can we learn from the order of Jesus' prayer so far?

7 // In this same verse, Jesus teaches us to ask for *daily bread*—just what we need for the day. How is praying this way an act of trust and dependency on God?

Let's dig into this idea a little more with a passage from the Old Testament. Read Exodus 16:13–21.

Mark the word *bread* (including the pronoun *it*) with a circle.

Exodus 16

13 In the evening quail came up and covered the camp, and in the morning dew lay around the camp.
14 And when the dew had gone up, there was on the face of the wilderness a fine, flake-like thing, fine as frost on the ground.
15 When the people of Israel saw it, they said to one another, "What is it?" For they did not know what it was. And Moses said to them, "It is the bread that the LORD has given you to eat.
16 This is what the LORD has commanded: 'Gather of it, each one of you, as much as he can eat. You shall each take an omer, according to the number of the persons that each of you has in his tent.'"
17 And the people of Israel did so. They gathered, some more, some less.
18 But when they measured it with an omer, whoever gathered much had nothing left over, and whoever gathered little had no lack. Each of them gathered as much as he could eat.
19 And Moses said to them, "Let no one leave any of it over till the morning."
20 But they did not listen to Moses. Some left part of it till the morning, and it bred worms and stank. And Moses was angry with them.
21 Morning by morning they gathered it, each as much as he could eat; but when the sun grew hot, it melted.

THE PURPOSE OF PRAYER

8 // How did the Lord provide for the Israelites in the wilderness?

9 // What did the Lord command about the gathering of the bread?

10 // In what way was God asking the Israelites to demonstrate trust and dependency on Him? How did they fail to do so?

11 // How does the Lord's provision for the Israelites in the wilderness relate to Jesus' prayer for daily bread?

Let's return to the Lord's Prayer in Matthew 6.

12 // In verse 12, we ask God to forgive us as we have forgiven others. Jesus expands on this in verses 14–15. Why is forgiveness an important part of our relationships with both God and others?

13 // Lastly, Jesus teaches us to pray against temptation and evil in verse 13. What does this show you about God's power over the evil and temptations in your life? How does this encourage you today?

14 // What would you like to incorporate from the Lord's Prayer into your daily prayers with God?

THE PURPOSE OF PRAYER

PRAY

Give thanks to Jesus for this beautiful example of prayer. Use this prayer to guide your own today. Perhaps you want to pray the words as written, pausing to meditate on each line. Or maybe you would like to personalize it into your own words, adding your requests along the way. Whatever you choose, seek your Father and give Him glory in your prayer time today.

A Collection on Prayer, Volume One

THE PURPOSE OF PRAYER

Lesson Nine: The Father Knows

MATTHEW 6

Jesus knew this life would be hard and come with its fair share of worries and anxieties. He addresses this in Matthew 6, pointing us to the love and care of our Father.

Read Matthew 6:25–34.

As you read, mark each of the following:

1 // references to *God* (including words like *Father* and *his*) with a purple triangle

2 // the word *anxious* with a blue underline

A Collection on Prayer, Volume One

⠿ Let's start with observation.

1 // Looking at your markings, what do you learn about God from Jesus' words? Make a list.

2 // What does Jesus say about us in comparison to the birds and the flowers?

3 // Look at verses 31–32. Why does Jesus tell us we are not to be anxious?

4 // What are we to do instead of dwelling on our worries and anxieties?

⠿ Reflect and Apply.

5 // What do Jesus' words show us about the Father's care for us?

THE **PURPOSE** OF PRAYER

6 // What things are causing you stress or anxiety in your life right now?

7 // Your Father knows your every need (verse 32). How does this make you feel? How could this truth change the way you approach your worries and anxieties?

8 // What does it look like for you to "seek first the kingdom of God" through prayer, especially in the midst of stress and anxiety?

Let's read another promise from Jesus. After His promise that the Father will send the Holy Spirit to dwell in us and be with us forever, Jesus spoke these words. Read John 14:27.

Mark the word *peace* with a circle.

> **John 14**
> 27 Peace I leave with you; my peace I give to you. Not as the world gives do I give to you. Let not your hearts be troubled, neither let them be afraid.

9 // What does Jesus promise to leave with us and to give us?

10 // How is the peace of Jesus meant to affect our hearts?

11 // In your experience, how has the peace of the world compared to the peace of Jesus?

12 // How can prayer remind you of the peace of Jesus, especially when worries and anxieties arise?

THE PURPOSE OF PRAYER

PRAY

Practice seeking God's kingdom first today by coming to Him in prayer. Before letting the worries and stresses of the day into your mind, surrender them to God. Before trying to accomplish or solve anything by your own strength, ask God for His. Before searching for the peace the world has to offer, remember that Jesus has given you His. Come to the Father with confidence, remembering that He knows your every need and cares for you. Write your prayer to Him below.

THE PURPOSE OF PRAYER

Lesson Ten: Prayer at a Glance

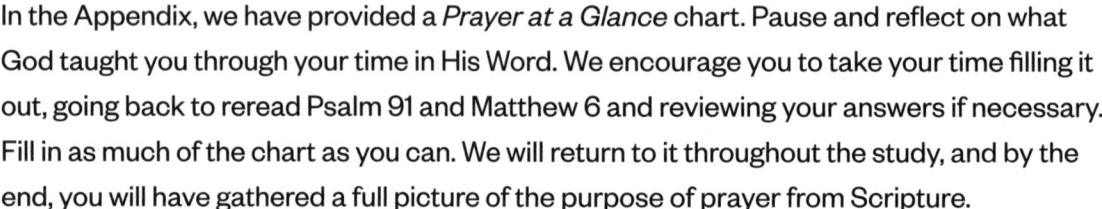

In the Appendix, we have provided a *Prayer at a Glance* chart. Pause and reflect on what God taught you through your time in His Word. We encourage you to take your time filling it out, going back to reread Psalm 91 and Matthew 6 and reviewing your answers if necessary. Fill in as much of the chart as you can. We will return to it throughout the study, and by the end, you will have gathered a full picture of the purpose of prayer from Scripture.

Pray without Ceasing

Spend some time over the next days and weeks committing the Lord's Prayer to memory (if you have not already). Memorizing Scripture is an important way to keep God's Word with us, and memorizing this prayer, in particular, reminds us to pray as Jesus did.

Take it one line at a time. You can repeat it to yourself, write it out, or place it somewhere you will see it every day. You can even use music—many songs have put the words of this prayer into melody. Choose a method that works best for you, and keep at it, using it as a way to grow in your relationship with your Father.

If you already have this prayer memorized, commit to thoughtfully praying it once a day, lifting your heart and requests to God through the words that Jesus taught us.

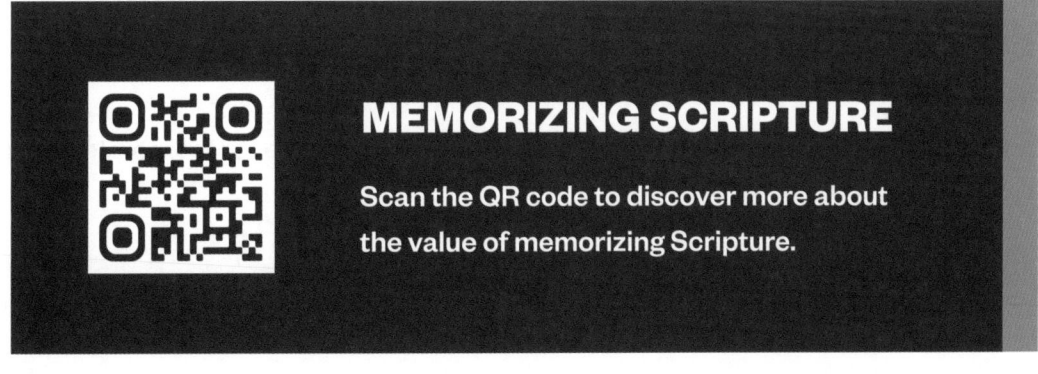

MEMORIZING SCRIPTURE

Scan the QR code to discover more about the value of memorizing Scripture.

THE PURPOSE OF PRAYER

WEEK TWO: GROUP DISCUSSION QUESTIONS

Opening Question: Begin by praying the Lord's Prayer out loud together. What line from the Lord's Prayer is currently speaking to you?

1 // **Observe and Apply** (Lesson 6, question 3, page 43): How would you describe the relationship between God and the person whom the psalmist is speaking about? What similarities do you see when you compare this to your relationship with God? In what areas would you like to grow in your relationship with Him?

Apply (Lesson 6, question 5, page 43): What other places do you find yourself running to from time to time—instead of the "shelter of the Most High" and "shadow of the Almighty"? Why do you think you turn to these places rather than God?

2 // **Observe** (Lesson 7, question 1, page 49): Contrast what Jesus says about the hypocrites and Gentiles and what He asks of His believers in Matthew 6. What is the main difference between the two?

Apply (Lesson 7, question 4, page 49): Where in your life do you sometimes struggle and act as the hypocrites and Gentiles? What earthly rewards tempt you to act in this way?

3 // **Observe and Interpret** (Lesson 8, question 3, page 56): What two words does this prayer begin with? Why is this significant?

Apply (Lesson 8, question 14, page 60): What would you like to incorporate from the Lord's Prayer into your daily prayers with God?

A Collection on Prayer, Volume One

4 // **Observe** (Lesson 9, question 4, page 64): According to Jesus' words in Matthew 6, what are we to do instead of dwelling on our worries and anxieties?

Apply (Lesson 9, questions 6 and 7, page 65): What things are causing you stress or anxiety in your life right now? Your Father knows your every need. How does this make you feel? How could this truth impact the way you approach your worries and anxieties?

5 // Prayer at a Glance (page 69): What did God teach you through your time in Psalm 91 and Matthew 6? What were your personal takeaways? How have these truths begun to impact your life?

Closing: End your time together by asking each member of your group to share their personal prayer requests. Then, spend time praying for one another. Commit to praying for each other throughout the week.

WEEK 2 WRAP-UP

Scan the QR code to listen to a roundtable discussion on what we have explored about prayer in Psalm 91 and Matthew 6.

A Collection on Prayer, Volume One

WEEK 3

Lesson Eleven: My Father

MATTHEW 26

Over the past two weeks, we have observed Jesus' intimate relationship with His Father. This week, we will continue to experience the depth of Their relationship. We will meet with Jesus in the middle of one of His most difficult moments—His time in the Garden of Gethsemane just before His arrest, trial, and death.

Read Matthew 26:36–46.

As you read, mark each of the following:

1 // the word *Father* with a purple triangle

2 // the word *pray* with a blue arrow pointing up

3 // references to time (such as *one hour* and *second time*) with a clock

It may help to read through the passage multiple times, marking each reference or word one at a time. Or, if you prefer, you can mark them all during a single read-through. Do what works best for you.

THE PURPOSE OF PRAYER

⋯ Let's begin with observation.

1 // Where does Jesus go in this passage?

2 // What does He do there?

3 // What does Jesus say to His Father?

4 // How many times does He pray these words to His Father?

5 // What happens at the end of Jesus' time in the garden?

Reflect and Apply.

6 // Jesus knew He only had a few hours left to live. Imagine you were in the same situation. How would you choose to spend those final moments?

7 // Reflect on the way Jesus spent His final moments before His betrayal and arrest. What does this reveal about His relationship with the Father?

8 // What do Jesus' words and actions teach us about the importance of prayer in His life?

9 // Jesus prays the same prayer to His Father three times while He is in the garden. What can we learn from His willingness to bring His request to the Father again and again?

10 // How did Jesus' time in prayer with the Father prepare Him for what He was about to endure?

THE PURPOSE OF PRAYER

Read John 14:31.

Jesus shared with His disciples the fate He will have to endure. And with these words, He told them why.

As you read, mark the word *Father* with a purple triangle.

> **John 14**
> 31 but I do as the Father has commanded me, so that the world may know that I love the Father. Rise, let us go from here.

11 // How does Jesus reveal His love of the Father to the world?

12 // How do Jesus' actions in Gethsemane demonstrate His love for the Father?

13 // How does your life—your words, thoughts, actions, and priorities—show evidence of your love for the Father?

14 // What does your prayer life reveal about your relationship with God?

15 // How can you begin seeking the kind of intimacy that Jesus has with His Father?

THE PURPOSE OF PRAYER

PRAY

Pour out your love for the Father in prayer today. Acknowledge His presence and nearness to you. Bring to Him your whole heart, honestly and authentically. Share the things that you haven't shared with Him before, trusting in His deep love and mercy.

THE PURPOSE OF PRAYER

Lesson Twelve: A Sorrowful Soul

MATTHEW 26

Jesus had always been fully God, perfectly One with His Father. When He came to earth, He also became fully human, taking on the full range of human experiences and emotions. Let's meet Him once again in the Garden of Gethsemane as we discover the intensity of His emotions and prayers in these hours.

Read Matthew 26:36–46.

As you read, mark the words *sorrowful* and *troubled* with a black underline.

Let's take a closer look.

1 // Whom does Jesus take with Him into the Garden of Gethsemane?

2 // How does Jesus describe His feelings to them in this moment?

3 // How does Jesus' experience in the garden show that He was fully human?

Let's read another account of this moment from the Gospel of Luke. Read Luke 22:44.

> **Luke 22**
> 44 And being in agony he prayed more earnestly; and his sweat became like great drops of blood falling down to the ground.

THE **PURPOSE** OF PRAYER

Reflect and Apply.

4 // How does the Gospel of Luke describe Jesus' feelings in this moment?

5 // What happened to Jesus as He was praying?

6 // The depth and intensity of Jesus' agony is clear. What does this reveal about what He is about to face?

7 // What did Jesus choose to do with His intense feelings of sorrow and anguish?

8 // According to Luke 22:44, how was Jesus praying?

A Collection on Prayer, Volume One

9 // These moments take place in Gethsemane, a garden originally covered in olive trees on the lower slopes of the Mount of Olives. The word *Gethsemane* means "oil press." Olives from the groves of trees were crushed for their oil. What is the significance of Jesus praying here before His death?

10 // What is your first response when you feel crushed by anxiety or troubles?

11 // Is there anything that keeps you from turning to God and earnestly praying in these moments, as Jesus did? If so, what is it?

Read Hebrews 4:15–16.

Hebrews 4

15 For we do not have a high priest who is unable to sympathize with our weaknesses, but one who in every respect has been tempted as we are, yet without sin.

16 Let us then with confidence draw near to the throne of grace, that we may receive mercy and find grace to help in time of need.

THE PURPOSE OF PRAYER

12 // How does the author of Hebrews describe Jesus?

13 // What are we now able to do because of what Jesus experienced? What do we receive there?

14 // How have you experienced the mercy and grace of God in your times of greatest need?

15 // How do these words, as well as Jesus' actions and prayers in the garden, encourage you in your own times of trouble?

16 // How can you remind yourself to make prayer your first response? How would it impact your life to live this way?

PRAY

Follow Jesus' humble and faithful example and come before the Father today in earnest and fervent prayer. Bring to Him anything in your life that feels challenging or overwhelming. Draw near to His throne of grace with confidence, trusting in His great mercy. Give thanks to Jesus for the compassion, understanding, and grace made available to you through His suffering and obedience.

Lesson Thirteen: As You Will

MATTHEW 28

Today we return to Jesus in the garden. We take a closer look at the words He prayed and His humble and obedient heart.

Read Matthew 26:36–46.

As you read, mark the word *will* with a double underline.

⋯ Let's take a closer look.

1 // What does Jesus ask of the Father each time He prays?

2 // How would you describe Jesus' prayer to the Father?

Read Jeremiah 25:15.

As you read, mark the word *cup* with a circle.

> **Jeremiah 25**
> 15 Thus the LORD, the God of Israel, said to me: "Take from my hand this cup of the wine of wrath, and make all the nations to whom I send you drink it.

3 // According to God's words to the prophet Jeremiah, what is in the Lord's cup?

THE PURPOSE OF PRAYER

4 // This is one example of many throughout the Old Testament where the cup is used as an image of the wrath and judgment of God. What is the significance of Jesus being asked to drink this cup?

5 // In Matthew 26, each time Jesus presents His request, what does He pray immediately afterwards?

6 // We know that God does not grant Jesus His request. Our Savior does end up drinking from the cup. What does this teach us about prayer?

7 // What do we learn about the heart of Jesus through His prayer, especially in a time of such deep sorrow and suffering?

Read Hebrews 5:7–9.

As you read, mark each of the following:

1 // references to *Jesus* (including words such as *his, him, he,* and *son*) with a red cross

2 // the words *obedience/obey* with a circle

> **Hebrews 5**
> 7   In the days of his flesh, Jesus offered up prayers and supplications, with loud cries and tears, to him who was able to save him from death, and he was heard because of his reverence.
> 8   Although he was a son, he learned obedience through what he suffered.
> 9   And being made perfect, he became the source of eternal salvation to all who obey him

8 // How did Jesus pray to the Father?

9 // How did God respond, and why did He respond this way?

10 // What was the result of Jesus' suffering?

THE PURPOSE OF PRAYER

11 // For whom is Jesus the source of eternal salvation?

12 // What can we learn from Jesus' suffering?

13 // Take a moment to consider some of the trials you have walked through in your life. How have you experienced "learning obedience through suffering"?

14 // Why is obedience of great importance in our relationship with the Father?

15 // Where in your life might God be challenging you to submit to His will? How can remembering Jesus' example of prayer and obedience in the garden help you to do so?

PRAY

Ask God where He might be calling you deeper into obedience. Seek to submit yourself to His will, in both the big and small things. Give thanks to Jesus for His beautiful example of humble obedience in the midst of suffering.

THE PURPOSE OF PRAYER

Lesson Fourteen: Winning the Battle through Prayer

MATTHEW 26

In our time with Jesus in the garden, we saw His profound sorrow and explored how He responded with humble obedience. Through it all, He revealed the depth of love and trust in His relationship with the Father. As we spend one final day with Jesus in Gethsemane, we will zoom out a bit to discover what His time here would come to mean for both His life and ours.

Slowly read Matthew 26:36–46 once more, as if for the first time.

A Collection on Prayer, Volume One

1 // What did Jesus ask His disciples to do?

2 // What did Jesus say to Peter after He returned and found them sleeping?

3 // How have you experienced the willingness of the spirit but the weakness of the flesh?

4 // How do Jesus' actions in the garden compare to those of the disciples?

5 // We know that later in the story, Peter will deny Jesus and His closest disciples will scatter and fall away. But Jesus will remain faithful and obedient to the very end. How does the disciples' prayer time in the garden relate to how they will respond to their various trials later?

6 // Prayer is essential to help us prepare for the spiritual battles ahead. How have you experienced this to be true in your own life?

THE PURPOSE OF PRAYER

Read Hebrews 2:17–18.

As you read, mark each of the following:

1 // references to *Jesus* (including pronouns such as *he, his,* and *himself*) with a red cross

2 // the word *tempted* with a circle

> **Hebrews 2**
>
> 17 Therefore he had to be made like his brothers in every respect, so that he might become a merciful and faithful high priest in the service of God, to make propitiation for the sins of the people.
> 18 For because he himself has suffered when tempted, he is able to help those who are being tempted.

7 // Why did Jesus have to be made human like us in every respect?

8 // What is the result of Jesus overcoming temptation?

9 // How can we follow Jesus' example of enduring temptation in the garden?

10 // What is the role of prayer in overcoming temptation?

11 // What might keep you from praying to Jesus in your moments of temptation and weakness?

12 // What are some truths you have gleaned from this study that encourage you to go to Jesus in your times of need? How can you continue to remind yourself of these truths?

THE PURPOSE OF PRAYER

PRAY

Give thanks and glory to Jesus for the way He overcame. Praise Him for the example He gave us of winning our battles through prayer. Thank Him for the help He provides for us to do the same. Bring to Him anything you may be struggling with today, trusting His understanding and the strength He brings you.

Lesson Fifteen: Prayer at a Glance

In the Appendix, we have provided a *Prayer at a Glance* chart. Pause and reflect on what God taught you through your time in His Word. We encourage you to take your time filling it out, going back to reread Matthew 26 and reviewing your answers if necessary. Fill in as much of the chart as you can. We will return to it throughout the study, and by the end, you will have gathered a full picture of the purpose of prayer from Scripture.

Pray without Ceasing

Jesus persevered in prayer during His time in the garden. Commit to doing the same as you go about the rest of your week.

Perhaps you gave up on a prayer long ago. Begin praying for this request again, asking God to renew your hope. Or maybe you find yourself in a season when prayer feels stale or stagnant. Consider changing up your prayer rhythms and connecting with God in a new way.

Reflect on what it might mean for you to persevere in prayer over the next few days and commit to doing so.

WEEK THREE: GROUP DISCUSSION QUESTIONS

Opening Questions: Who has been a faithful and supportive friend to you during a hard time in your life?

1 // **Observe and Interpret** (Lesson 11, question 7, page 78): Reflect on the way Jesus spent His final moments before His betrayal and arrest. What does this reveal to us about His relationship with the Father?

Apply (Lesson 11, question 15, page 80): How can you begin to seek the kind of intimacy that Jesus has with His Father?

2 // **Observe and Interpret** (Lesson 12, question 3, page 84): How does Jesus' experience in the garden show that He was fully human?

Apply (Lesson 12, question 11, page 86): Is there anything that keeps you from turning to God and earnestly praying when you are feeling overwhelmed, anxious, or troubled, as Jesus did? If so, what is it?

3 // **Observe and Interpret** (Lesson 13, questions 1 and 2, page 90): What does Jesus ask of the Father each time He prays? How would you describe Jesus' prayer to the Father?

Apply (Lesson 13, question 15, page 93): Where in your life might God be challenging you to submit to His will? How can remembering Jesus' example of prayer and obedience in the garden help you to do so?

THE **PURPOSE** OF PRAYER

4 // **Observe and Interpret** (Lesson 14, questions 4 and 10, pages 96 and 98): How do Jesus' actions in the garden compare to those of the disciples? What is the role of prayer in overcoming temptation?

Apply (Lesson 14, question 12, page 98): What are some truths you have gleaned from this study that encourage you to go to Jesus in your times of need? How can you continue to remind yourself of these truths?

5 // Prayer at a Glance (page 101): What did God teach you through your time in Matthew 26? What were your personal takeaways? How have the truths of Matthew 26 begun to impact your life?

Closing: End your time together by asking each member of your group to share their personal prayer requests. Then, spend time praying for one another. Commit to praying for each other throughout the week.

WEEK 3 WRAP-UP

Scan the QR code to listen to a roundtable discussion on what we have explored about prayer in Matthew 26.

A Collection on Prayer, Volume One

WEEK 4

Lesson Sixteen: History with God

DANIEL 1

We are turning our attention to the prophet Daniel. As you read and reflect, notice Daniel's faithfulness to God, but even more so, God's faithfulness to Daniel.

The Context

The book of Daniel takes place during the time of Judah's Babylonian captivity. Daniel and his friends are among those brought to Babylon by King Nebuchadnezzar. Daniel's ministry begins here. His message encourages the Jewish exiles, reminding them of God's sovereignty and inspiring them to remain faithful to God, even in the midst of difficult circumstances.

THE PURPOSE OF PRAYER

Read Daniel 1.

In the Appendix, you will find an Observation Sheet with the text of Daniel 1.

As you read, mark each of the following:

1 // references to time (such as the *third year* or the *end of time*) with a clock

2 // references to *Daniel* and his friends (including pronouns such as *he, you,* and *they*) with an orange box

3 // the phrase *God gave* with a purple triangle

4 // the word *defile* with an underline

5 // the word *better* with a double underline

It may help to read through the passage multiple times, marking each reference or word one at a time. Or, if you prefer, you can mark them all during a single read-through. Do what works best for you.

Let's begin with some of our observation questions—*who, what, when, where, why,* and *how*.

1 // When does this part of Daniel's story take place?

2 // Who was the king of Babylon? What did he do?

3 // What do you learn about Daniel and his friends in this chapter? Use your markings to make a list.

4 // Why did Daniel choose not to eat the king's food or drink the king's wine?

Note: While this passage does not specify the reason the food and drink were defiled, it is likely that they had been sacrificed to idols and did not adhere to the Jewish dietary laws found in Leviticus 11. By making this choice, Daniel was choosing obedience to God.

5 // What was the result of Daniel's obedience?

6 // What do Daniel's actions show us about his relationship with God?

7 // How do we see God's faithfulness to Daniel throughout this chapter?

8 // How were Daniel and his friends able to remain faithful to God?

THE PURPOSE OF PRAYER

Read Matthew 15:10–11, 16–20.

Although God still calls us to faithfulness and obedience today, it is no longer food that defiles us. Let's explore what Jesus says about this.

As you read, mark the word *defile* with a circle.

> **Matthew 15**
> 10 And he called the people to him and said to them, "Hear and understand:
> 11 it is not what goes into the mouth that defiles a person, but what comes out of the mouth; this defiles a person."
> . . .
> 16 And he said, "Are you also still without understanding?
> 17 Do you not see that whatever goes into the mouth passes into the stomach and is expelled?
> 18 But what comes out of the mouth proceeds from the heart, and this defiles a person.
> 19 For out of the heart come evil thoughts, murder, adultery, sexual immorality, theft, false witness, slander.
> 20 These are what defile a person. But to eat with unwashed hands does not defile anyone."

9 // According to Jesus, what does *not* defile a person?

10 // What *does* defile a person? List the examples that Jesus gives.

11 // According to Jesus' words, how can we continue to be faithful and obedient to Him today as Daniel was in his day?

12 // Jesus tells us that "what comes out of the mouth proceeds from the heart." How does the state of our hearts impact the way we pray and relate to God?

13 // Daniel chose obedience and faithfulness to God even when his circumstances tempted him to act differently. Jesus prayed regarding temptation in the Lord's Prayer in Matthew 6. He faced and overcame temptation in the garden in Matthew 26.

After reflecting on these truths, what things tempt you away from obedience and faithfulness to God in your own life? How do these examples encourage you to remain obedient and faithful in the face of temptation?

THE PURPOSE OF PRAYER

14 // Daniel made a courageous and obedient choice. Oftentimes these choices are not made in the moment, but rather flow out of years of prayer and relationship with God. How do prayer and faithfulness go hand in hand? Where have you seen this to be true in your own life?

15 // What is an area of your life where you struggle to remain faithful and obedient to God? How might it help to remember God's faithfulness to you?

PRAY

Daniel's history and experience with God enabled him to step out in bold faithfulness. Creating your own history with God starts by simply showing up to be with Him day after day. Come to Him today, giving Him thanks and glory for His faithfulness to you. Ask Him for the grace to remain faithful and obedient through any of life's challenges you may be facing. Write your prayer to Him below.

A Collection on Prayer, Volume One

THE PURPOSE OF PRAYER

Lesson Seventeen: God Comes Through

DANIEL 2

In the previous chapter, we caught a glimpse of Daniel's relationship with God—his faithfulness toward God and God's even greater faithfulness toward him. As we pick up Daniel's story today, we will see this continue, even as Daniel's life is threatened.

Read Daniel 2.

In the Appendix, you will find an Observation Sheet with the text of Daniel 2.

As you read, mark each of the following:
- **1 //** references to time (such as the *second year* and the *latter days*) with a clock
- **2 //** references to *Daniel* (including pronouns such as *he, his, I,* and *me*) with an orange box
- **3 //** references to *God* (including pronouns such as *he, him,* and *you*) with a purple triangle
- **4 //** the word *dream* with an underline
- **5 //** the word *interpretation* with a double underline

It may help to read through the passage multiple times, marking each reference or word one at a time. Or, if you prefer, you can mark them all during a single read-through. Do what works best for you.

Let's take a closer look.

1 // When does this part of Daniel's story take place?

2 // What is King Nebuchadnezzar's request? What will happen if it is not fulfilled?

3 // How do the Chaldeans (another name for the Babylonians) respond? *Pay special attention to verse 11.*

4 // What does Daniel do in verse 16?

5 // What does Daniel do in verses 17–18? What do Daniel and his friends request from God specifically?

THE PURPOSE OF PRAYER

6 // What does the order of these events show about Daniel's relationship with God and what he believed about Him?

7 // How was God faithful to Daniel?

8 // How does Daniel respond to God in return?

9 // Look at Daniel's prayer to God in verses 20-23. List each attribute Daniel declares about God.

10 // Once Daniel is before the king, to whom does he give credit? What does he declare about God?

Reflect and Apply.

11 // Looking at the list you made in question 9, what aspects of God's character are highlighted in this passage? What do we learn about who God is and what only He can do?

12 // What do we learn from Daniel about responding to life's challenges and difficult circumstances?

Reflect on a challenging circumstance you are facing in your life right now.

13 // Describe the circumstance below. What is going on? How are you feeling about it? How have you been dealing with it or praying about it?

14 // In what ways would you like to respond more faithfully and prayerfully to the circumstance you are facing? What is a step you can take to begin responding in this way?

15 // What aspect of God's character from today's passage encourages you in the middle of your circumstance? How can you continue to remind yourself of this?

THE PURPOSE OF PRAYER

PRAY

Daniel gave us examples of . . .
wisdom in the face of a challenge,
prayer in view of a problem,
and praise in response to God's faithfulness.

Seek God in such a way . . .
asking Him for wisdom where you need it,
offering your heart to Him in prayer,
and praising Him for always being good and faithful.

THE PURPOSE OF PRAYER

Lesson Eighteen: But If Not . . .

DANIEL 3

We have seen God's great faithfulness in answering the prayers of Daniel and his friends. But what if God hadn't answered? Is He still faithful then? Today we turn our attention to Daniel's three friends—Shadrach, Meshach, and Abednego—to hear their faithful response to this question.

Read Daniel 3.

In the Appendix, you will find an Observation Sheet with the text of Daniel 3.

As you read, mark references to *God* (including pronouns such as *he, his,* and *him*) with a purple triangle.

Let's take a closer look with some observation questions.

1 // What did King Nebuchadnezzar command his people? What would happen to anyone who did not obey his orders?

2 // Why did Shadrach, Meshach, and Abednego refuse to obey the king's decree?

3 // What does their refusal show about their relationship with God and faithfulness toward Him?

Underline the phrase *but if not* in verse 18.

4 // What did Shadrach, Meshach, and Abednego say to King Nebuchadnezzar in verses 17–18? Summarize in your own words.

5 // In light of this statement, what did these men believe about God?

6 // How do we see God's faithfulness in this passage?

THE **PURPOSE** OF PRAYER

Read Isaiah 43:1–3.

As you read, mark references to *Israel* (including the words *you* and *Jacob*) with a circle.

> **Isaiah 43**
> 1 But now thus says the LORD,
>   he who created you, O Jacob,
>   he who formed you, O Israel:
>   "Fear not, for I have redeemed you;
>   I have called you by name, you are mine.
> 2 When you pass through the waters, I will be with you;
>   and through the rivers, they shall not overwhelm you;
>   when you walk through fire you shall not be burned,
>   and the flame shall not consume you.
> 3 For I am the LORD your God,
>   the Holy One of Israel, your Savior . . .

7 // Who does God declare Himself to be to Israel—and to us?

8 // What does He promise to do when we pass through the waters, rivers, or fire?

9 // How does God stay true to His word through the story of Shadrach, Meshach, and Abednego?

10 // Not only does God deliver Shadrach, Meshach, and Abednego from the fire, but He is also with them in the fire. How does this truth that God is with you, even in your most difficult circumstances, encourage you today?

11 // In this story, God rescued Shadrach, Meshach, and Abednego from the fire. But we know that this isn't always the case. Reflect on one of your prayers that was not answered in the way you had hoped. Or perhaps reflect on a prayer that remains unanswered. How does your perspective shift when you remember that God is still with you in the midst of the fire? How can you continue to remind yourself of this truth?

12 // Prayer is not simply a means of getting what we want, but rather a way of growing in intimacy with our Father. How do Shadrach, Meshach, and Abednego's words and actions show us this?

13 // How would it transform your life and your relationship with God to treat prayer this way?

THE PURPOSE OF PRAYER

PRAY

Thank God for being with you and for His great faithfulness. Take a moment to simply rest in the truth of who He is. Then, lift up your answer to question 11 in prayer to God. Share with Him your heart, feelings, doubts, and questions, knowing that He isn't surprised by any of them. Ask Him for the faith and the trust you need to truly believe that even when He doesn't do what you know He can do, He is still God, and He is still good.

A Collection on Prayer, Volume One

Lesson Nineteen: Draw Near

JAMES 4

Together we read Jesus' teachings on abiding and prayer. We also saw Daniel's example of faithfulness to God through prayer and obedience. Now, we will turn to James' letter and read his instructions, for both his original audience and us today.

Read James 4.

In the Appendix, you will find an Observation Sheet with the text of James 4.

As you read, mark each of the following:

1 // references to *God* (including the pronoun *he*) with a purple triangle

2 // references to James' audience (including pronouns such as *you* and *your*) with an orange box

3 // the phrase *do not* with a red underline

4 // the word *ask* with an arrow pointing up

It may help to read through the passage multiple times, marking each reference or word one at a time. Or, if you prefer, you can mark them all during a single read-through. Do what works best for you.

Let's take a closer look.

1 // According to James, why do we not "have"?

2 // Why do we not "receive"?

3 // What happens if we pursue our passions? How does this cause relational strife? How does it impact the way we pray?

4 // Rather than praying with selfish motives, how are we to come before God and pray?

5 // What role does humility play in both our relationship with God and our prayers to Him?

6 // What does James invite us to do toward God in verse 8? What does God promise if we do this?

THE PURPOSE OF PRAYER

Reflect and Apply.

7 // What keeps you from asking God for things in prayer? How does this passage encourage you to ask?

8 // How can you pray to God humbly and with the right motives? How might seeking God's will help with this?

9 // God promises to draw near to us when we draw near to Him. What does this reveal about His heart for us?

Read Hebrews 11:6.

As you read, mark the phrase *draw near* with a circle.

> **Hebrews 11**
> 6 And without faith it is impossible to please him, for whoever would draw near to God must believe that he exists and that he rewards those who seek him.

10 // What is impossible to do without faith? Why?

11 // How do faith in God and drawing near to Him go hand in hand?

12 // How can prayer help us draw near to God?

13 // What are some practical ways you can commit to drawing near to God this week?

THE PURPOSE OF PRAYER

PRAY

Give thanks and praise to God for being a Father who delights in your company and friendship. Come before Him with a pure and humble heart, asking for the grace to do so. Practice drawing near to Him throughout your day, remembering that as you draw near to Him, He draws near to you.

Lesson Twenty: Prayer at a Glance

In the Appendix, we have provided a *Prayer at a Glance* chart. Pause and reflect on what God taught you through your time in His Word. We encourage you to take your time filling it out, going back to reread Daniel 1–3 and James 4 and reviewing your answers if necessary. Fill in as much of the chart as you can. By the end of our study, you will have gathered a full picture of the purpose of prayer from Scripture.

Pause and Reflect

We explored some difficult topics during our time in the books of Daniel and James. Let's slow down and process our thoughts and emotions through journaling. We have listed some journaling prompts to get you thinking. Feel free to reflect on all of these or just the ones that stand out to you. You can spend time on them today or take them one at a time over the next few days. Do what works best for you, seeking God in your reflection and writing.

1 // Paul reminds us that *"if we are faithless, he remains faithful…"* (2 Timothy 2:13). Do you believe this to be true? In what ways do you believe or live like you need to earn God's faithfulness on your own?

2 // Reread Daniel's prayer in Daniel 2:20–23. What stands out to you about his prayer? What do you learn from Daniel and his prayer about responding to God's faithfulness in your life? How can you give God glory and praise today?

3 // Daniel and his friends stood strong in their faith, even to the point of death. While we may not live in a culture that is threatening our lives, it can still be challenging to boldly live out our faith in today's world. Where do you experience these challenges in your life? What would it look like for you to boldly choose faith and obedience to God? What can help you to do so?

4 // After witnessing Shadrach, Meshach, and Abednego's faith, King Nebuchadnezzar blesses God and believes. How has the faithfulness and obedience of others inspired your faith? How might your faithfulness and obedience to God draw others to Him?

5 // James 4 teaches us that "friendship with the world is enmity with God." In what areas of your life do you find yourself choosing friendship with the world over friendship with God? What would it take for you to overcome this and choose God instead?

Pray without Ceasing

In Daniel 2, Daniel invited his friends to pray alongside him. Having people around to help us navigate the challenges of life is important. This is one of the many reasons God has given us the gift of community.

Reach out to a friend and ask how you can pray alongside them. Connect something from your daily routine to remind you to pray for them. *For example, if they are a voracious reader, allow the sight of books to remind you to lift them up in prayer.* Commit to praying for them often throughout your week.

THE **PURPOSE** OF PRAYER

WEEK FOUR: GROUP DISCUSSION QUESTIONS

Opening Question: Describe a time you demonstrated faithfulness to God when it wasn't easy to do so.

1 // Observe and Interpret (Lesson 16, question 6, page 110): What do Daniel's actions in Daniel 1 show us about his relationship with God?

Apply (Lesson 16, question 15, page 113): What is an area of your life where you struggle to remain faithful and obedient to God? How might it help to remember God's faithfulness to you?

2 // Observe (Lesson 17, questions 7 and 8, page 117): How was God faithful to Daniel throughout Daniel 2? And how does Daniel respond to God in return?

Apply (Lesson 17, question 15, page 118): What aspect of God's character that you read about in Daniel 2 encourages you in the middle of your challenging circumstance? How can you continue to remind yourself of this?

3 // Observe and Interpret (Lesson 18, questions 4 and 5, page 122): What did Shadrach, Meshach, and Abednego say to King Nebuchadnezzar in Daniel 3:17–18? Summarize in your own words. In light of this statement, what did these men believe about God?

Interpret and Apply (Lesson 18, questions 12 and 13, page 124): Prayer is not simply a means of getting what we want, but rather a way of growing in intimacy with our Father. How do Shadrach, Meshach, and Abednego's words and actions show us this? How would it transform your life and your relationship with God to treat prayer this way?

THE PURPOSE OF PRAYER

4 // ⫶ **Interpret** (Lesson 19, question 9, page 129): God promises to draw near to us when we draw near to Him. What does this reveal about His heart for us?

⫶ **Apply** (Lesson 19, question 13, page 130): What are some practical ways you can commit to drawing near to God this week?

5 // Prayer at a Glance (page 133): What did God teach you through your time in Daniel 1–3 and James 4? What were your personal takeaways? How have the truths of these chapters begun to impact your life?

Pause and Reflect (page 133): Which of these questions stood out as particularly meaningful to you? What were some of your reflections?

Closing: End your time together by asking each member of your group to share their personal prayer requests. Then, spend time praying for one another. Commit to praying for each other throughout the week.

WEEK 4 WRAP-UP

Scan the QR code to listen to a roundtable discussion on what we have explored about prayer in Daniel 1-3 and James 4.

A Collection on Prayer, Volume One

Conclusion

We have journeyed through the Bible—to John, Psalms, Matthew, Daniel, and James—in search of the purpose of prayer. As we wrap up our time together, let's take a step back and retrace the thread we have been following. Our goal is to understand the Bible as one full story, seeing how it fits together and how our own stories intersect with God's story.

Begin by reviewing your *Prayer at a Glance* chart. Feel free to add or change anything. When you are finished, continue to the questions below.

1 // Has your reason for praying changed since beginning this study? If yes, how?

2 // Have your prayer life and rhythms changed since beginning this study? If yes, how?

3 // How has your relationship with God grown or changed during your time in Scripture?

4 // What truths and takeaways stand out to you from your time of study?

5 // How would living in light of the truths you have discovered about prayer impact your life and your relationship with God?

Father,

Thank You for Your presence.
Thank You for the gift of relationship with You.
Thank You for the ability to draw near.

I recognize that I am so undeserving of
Your mercy,
Your grace,
Your love,
Your friendship.
Yet You give it all away so freely to me through Your Son, Jesus.

I am humbled to call You my Father.

Help my wandering heart
to draw near to You,
to desire You,
to return to You often in prayer,
in thanksgiving,
and communion.

I love You.
And I thank You for loving me.

Amen.

CLOSING GROUP DISCUSSION QUESTIONS

As you wrap up your time in this study together, discuss your answers and reflections from the Conclusion chapter on page 139 of your study.

Opening Question: What surprised you the most from your time in this study or in this group?

1 // Has your reason for praying changed at all since beginning this study? If yes, how?

2 // Has your prayer life or rhythms changed since beginning this study? If yes, how?

3 // How has your relationship with God grown or changed during your time in Scripture?

4 // What truths and takeaways stand out to you from your time of study?

5 // How would living in light of the truths you have discovered about prayer impact your life and your relationship with God?

Closing: End your time together by asking each member of your group to share their personal prayer requests. Then, spend time praying for one another. Commit to praying for each other even beyond your time in this group.

A Collection on Prayer, Volume One

Appendix

OBSERVATION SHEETS

All bolded Scripture numbers represent a paragraph break.

OBSERVATION SHEET

John 15

1 "I am the true vine, and my Father is the vinedresser.
2 Every branch in me that does not bear fruit he takes away, and every branch that does bear fruit he prunes, that it may bear more fruit.
3 Already you are clean because of the word that I have spoken to you.
4 Abide in me, and I in you. As the branch cannot bear fruit by itself, unless it abides in the vine, neither can you, unless you abide in me.
5 I am the vine; you are the branches. Whoever abides in me and I in him, he it is that bears much fruit, for apart from me you can do nothing.
6 If anyone does not abide in me he is thrown away like a branch and withers; and the branches are gathered, thrown into the fire, and burned.
7 If you abide in me, and my words abide in you, ask whatever you wish, and it will be done for you.
8 By this my Father is glorified, that you bear much fruit and so prove to be my disciples.
9 As the Father has loved me, so have I loved you. Abide in my love.
10 If you keep my commandments, you will abide in my love, just as I have kept my Father's commandments and abide in his love.
11 These things I have spoken to you, that my joy may be in you, and that your joy may be full.
12 "This is my commandment, that you love one another as I have loved you.
13 Greater love has no one than this, that someone lay down his life for his friends.
14 You are my friends if you do what I command you.
15 No longer do I call you servants, for the servant does not know what his master is doing; but I have called you friends, for all that I have heard from my Father I have made known to you.
16 You did not choose me, but I chose you and appointed you that you should go and bear fruit and that your fruit should abide, so that whatever you ask the Father in my name, he may give it to you.
17 These things I command you, so that you will love one another.

APPENDIX: OBSERVATION SHEETS

OBSERVATION SHEET

Psalm 91

1 He who dwells in the shelter of the Most High
   will abide in the shadow of the Almighty.
2 I will say to the LORD, "My refuge and my fortress,
   my God, in whom I trust."
3 For he will deliver you from the snare of the fowler
   and from the deadly pestilence.
4 He will cover you with his pinions,
   and under his wings you will find refuge;
   his faithfulness is a shield and buckler.
5 You will not fear the terror of the night,
   nor the arrow that flies by day,
6 nor the pestilence that stalks in darkness,
   nor the destruction that wastes at noonday.
7 A thousand may fall at your side,
   ten thousand at your right hand,
   but it will not come near you.
8 You will only look with your eyes
   and see the recompense of the wicked.
9 Because you have made the LORD your dwelling place—
   the Most High, who is my refuge—
10 no evil shall be allowed to befall you,
   no plague come near your tent.
11 For he will command his angels concerning you
   to guard you in all your ways.
12 On their hands they will bear you up,
   lest you strike your foot against a stone.
13 You will tread on the lion and the adder;
   the young lion and the serpent you will trample underfoot.
14 "Because he holds fast to me in love, I will deliver him;
   I will protect him, because he knows my name.

15 When he calls to me, I will answer him;
    I will be with him in trouble;
    I will rescue him and honor him.
16 With long life I will satisfy him
    and show him my salvation."

APPENDIX: OBSERVATION SHEETS

OBSERVATION SHEET

Matthew 6

1. Beware of practicing your righteousness before other people in order to be seen by them, for then you will have no reward from your Father who is in heaven.
2. "Thus, when you give to the needy, sound no trumpet before you, as the hypocrites do in the synagogues and in the streets, that they may be praised by others. Truly, I say to you, they have received their reward.
3. But when you give to the needy, do not let your left hand know what your right hand is doing,
4. so that your giving may be in secret. And your Father who sees in secret will reward you.
5. "And when you pray, you must not be like the hypocrites. For they love to stand and pray in the synagogues and at the street corners, that they may be seen by others. Truly, I say to you, they have received their reward.
6. But when you pray, go into your room and shut the door and pray to your Father who is in secret. And your Father who sees in secret will reward you.
7. "And when you pray, do not heap up empty phrases as the Gentiles do, for they think that they will be heard for their many words.
8. Do not be like them, for your Father knows what you need before you ask him.
9. Pray then like this:
   "Our Father in heaven,
   hallowed be your name.
10. Your kingdom come,
    your will be done,
       on earth as it is in heaven.
11. Give us this day our daily bread,
12. and forgive us our debts,
       as we also have forgiven our debtors.
13. And lead us not into temptation,
       but deliver us from evil.

14 For if you forgive others their trespasses, your heavenly Father will also forgive you,
15 but if you do not forgive others their trespasses, neither will your Father forgive your trespasses.
16 "And when you fast, do not look gloomy like the hypocrites, for they disfigure their faces that their fasting may be seen by others. Truly, I say to you, they have received their reward.
17 But when you fast, anoint your head and wash your face,
18 that your fasting may not be seen by others but by your Father who is in secret. And your Father who sees in secret will reward you.
19 "Do not lay up for yourselves treasures on earth, where moth and rust destroy and where thieves break in and steal,
20 but lay up for yourselves treasures in heaven, where neither moth nor rust destroys and where thieves do not break in and steal.
21 For where your treasure is, there your heart will be also.
22 "The eye is the lamp of the body. So, if your eye is healthy, your whole body will be full of light,
23 but if your eye is bad, your whole body will be full of darkness. If then the light in you is darkness, how great is the darkness!
24 "No one can serve two masters, for either he will hate the one and love the other, or he will be devoted to the one and despise the other. You cannot serve God and money.
25 "Therefore I tell you, do not be anxious about your life, what you will eat or what you will drink, nor about your body, what you will put on. Is not life more than food, and the body more than clothing?
26 Look at the birds of the air: they neither sow nor reap nor gather into barns, and yet your heavenly Father feeds them. Are you not of more value than they?
27 And which of you by being anxious can add a single hour to his span of life?
28 And why are you anxious about clothing? Consider the lilies of the field, how they grow: they neither toil nor spin,

APPENDIX: OBSERVATION SHEETS

29 yet I tell you, even Solomon in all his glory was not arrayed like one of these.

30 But if God so clothes the grass of the field, which today is alive and tomorrow is thrown into the oven, will he not much more clothe you, O you of little faith?

31 Therefore do not be anxious, saying, 'What shall we eat?' or 'What shall we drink?' or 'What shall we wear?'

32 For the Gentiles seek after all these things, and your heavenly Father knows that you need them all.

33 But seek first the kingdom of God and his righteousness, and all these things will be added to you.

34 "Therefore do not be anxious about tomorrow, for tomorrow will be anxious for itself. Sufficient for the day is its own trouble.

OBSERVATION SHEET

Matthew 26:36–46

36 Then Jesus went with them to a place called Gethsemane, and he said to his disciples, "Sit here, while I go over there and pray."

37 And taking with him Peter and the two sons of Zebedee, he began to be sorrowful and troubled.

38 Then he said to them, "My soul is very sorrowful, even to death; remain here, and watch with me."

39 And going a little farther he fell on his face and prayed, saying, "My Father, if it be possible, let this cup pass from me; nevertheless, not as I will, but as you will."

40 And he came to the disciples and found them sleeping. And he said to Peter, "So, could you not watch with me one hour?

41 Watch and pray that you may not enter into temptation. The spirit indeed is willing, but the flesh is weak."

42 Again, for the second time, he went away and prayed, "My Father, if this cannot pass unless I drink it, your will be done."

43 And again he came and found them sleeping, for their eyes were heavy.

44 So, leaving them again, he went away and prayed for the third time, saying the same words again.

45 Then he came to the disciples and said to them, "Sleep and take your rest later on. See, the hour is at hand, and the Son of Man is betrayed into the hands of sinners.

46 Rise, let us be going; see, my betrayer is at hand."

APPENDIX: OBSERVATION SHEETS

OBSERVATION SHEET

Daniel 1

1 In the third year of the reign of Jehoiakim king of Judah, Nebuchadnezzar king of Babylon came to Jerusalem and besieged it.
2 And the Lord gave Jehoiakim king of Judah into his hand, with some of the vessels of the house of God. And he brought them to the land of Shinar, to the house of his god, and placed the vessels in the treasury of his god.
3 Then the king commanded Ashpenaz, his chief eunuch, to bring some of the people of Israel, both of the royal family and of the nobility,
4 youths without blemish, of good appearance and skillful in all wisdom, endowed with knowledge, understanding learning, and competent to stand in the king's palace, and to teach them the literature and language of the Chaldeans.
5 The king assigned them a daily portion of the food that the king ate, and of the wine that he drank. They were to be educated for three years, and at the end of that time they were to stand before the king.
6 Among these were Daniel, Hananiah, Mishael, and Azariah of the tribe of Judah.
7 And the chief of the eunuchs gave them names: Daniel he called Belteshazzar, Hananiah he called Shadrach, Mishael he called Meshach, and Azariah he called Abednego.
8 But Daniel resolved that he would not defile himself with the king's food, or with the wine that he drank. Therefore he asked the chief of the eunuchs to allow him not to defile himself.
9 And God gave Daniel favor and compassion in the sight of the chief of the eunuchs,
10 and the chief of the eunuchs said to Daniel, "I fear my lord the king, who assigned your food and your drink; for why should he see that you were in worse condition than the youths who are of your own age? So you would endanger my head with the king."
11 Then Daniel said to the steward whom the chief of the eunuchs had assigned over Daniel, Hananiah, Mishael, and Azariah,

12 "Test your servants for ten days; let us be given vegetables to eat and water to drink.
13 Then let our appearance and the appearance of the youths who eat the king's food be observed by you, and deal with your servants according to what you see."
14 So he listened to them in this matter, and tested them for ten days.
15 At the end of ten days it was seen that they were better in appearance and fatter in flesh than all the youths who ate the king's food.
16 So the steward took away their food and the wine they were to drink, and gave them vegetables.
17 As for these four youths, God gave them learning and skill in all literature and wisdom, and Daniel had understanding in all visions and dreams.
18 At the end of the time, when the king had commanded that they should be brought in, the chief of the eunuchs brought them in before Nebuchadnezzar.
19 And the king spoke with them, and among all of them none was found like Daniel, Hananiah, Mishael, and Azariah. Therefore they stood before the king.
20 And in every matter of wisdom and understanding about which the king inquired of them, he found them ten times better than all the magicians and enchanters that were in all his kingdom.
21 And Daniel was there until the first year of King Cyrus.

APPENDIX: **OBSERVATION SHEETS**

OBSERVATION SHEET

Daniel 2

1 In the second year of the reign of Nebuchadnezzar, Nebuchadnezzar had dreams; his spirit was troubled, and his sleep left him.

2 Then the king commanded that the magicians, the enchanters, the sorcerers, and the Chaldeans be summoned to tell the king his dreams. So they came in and stood before the king.

3 And the king said to them, "I had a dream, and my spirit is troubled to know the dream."

4 Then the Chaldeans said to the king in Aramaic, "O king, live forever! Tell your servants the dream, and we will show the interpretation."

5 The king answered and said to the Chaldeans, "The word from me is firm: if you do not make known to me the dream and its interpretation, you shall be torn limb from limb, and your houses shall be laid in ruins.

6 But if you show the dream and its interpretation, you shall receive from me gifts and rewards and great honor. Therefore show me the dream and its interpretation."

7 They answered a second time and said, "Let the king tell his servants the dream, and we will show its interpretation."

8 The king answered and said, "I know with certainty that you are trying to gain time, because you see that the word from me is firm—

9 if you do not make the dream known to me, there is but one sentence for you. You have agreed to speak lying and corrupt words before me till the times change. Therefore tell me the dream, and I shall know that you can show me its interpretation."

10 The Chaldeans answered the king and said, "There is not a man on earth who can meet the king's demand, for no great and powerful king has asked such a thing of any magician or enchanter or Chaldean.

11 The thing that the king asks is difficult, and no one can show it to the king except the gods, whose dwelling is not with flesh."

12 Because of this the king was angry and very furious, and commanded that all the wise men of Babylon be destroyed.

13 So the decree went out, and the wise men were about to be killed; and they sought Daniel and his companions, to kill them.
14 Then Daniel replied with prudence and discretion to Arioch, the captain of the king's guard, who had gone out to kill the wise men of Babylon.
15 He declared to Arioch, the king's captain, "Why is the decree of the king so urgent?" Then Arioch made the matter known to Daniel.
16 And Daniel went in and requested the king to appoint him a time, that he might show the interpretation to the king.
17 Then Daniel went to his house and made the matter known to Hananiah, Mishael, and Azariah, his companions,
18 and told them to seek mercy from the God of heaven concerning this mystery, so that Daniel and his companions might not be destroyed with the rest of the wise men of Babylon.
19 Then the mystery was revealed to Daniel in a vision of the night. Then Daniel blessed the God of heaven.
20 Daniel answered and said:

"Blessed be the name of God forever and ever,
    to whom belong wisdom and might.
21 He changes times and seasons;
    he removes kings and sets up kings;
he gives wisdom to the wise
    and knowledge to those who have understanding;
22 he reveals deep and hidden things;
    he knows what is in the darkness,
    and the light dwells with him.
23 To you, O God of my fathers,
    I give thanks and praise,
for you have given me wisdom and might,
    and have now made known to me what we asked of you,
    for you have made known to us the king's matter."

APPENDIX: OBSERVATION SHEETS

24 Therefore Daniel went in to Arioch, whom the king had appointed to destroy the wise men of Babylon. He went and said thus to him: "Do not destroy the wise men of Babylon; bring me in before the king, and I will show the king the interpretation."

25 Then Arioch brought in Daniel before the king in haste and said thus to him: "I have found among the exiles from Judah a man who will make known to the king the interpretation."

26 The king declared to Daniel, whose name was Belteshazzar, "Are you able to make known to me the dream that I have seen and its interpretation?"

27 Daniel answered the king and said, "No wise men, enchanters, magicians, or astrologers can show to the king the mystery that the king has asked,

28 but there is a God in heaven who reveals mysteries, and he has made known to King Nebuchadnezzar what will be in the latter days. Your dream and the visions of your head as you lay in bed are these:

29 To you, O king, as you lay in bed came thoughts of what would be after this, and he who reveals mysteries made known to you what is to be.

30 But as for me, this mystery has been revealed to me, not because of any wisdom that I have more than all the living, but in order that the interpretation may be made known to the king, and that you may know the thoughts of your mind.

OBSERVATION SHEET

Daniel 3

1 King Nebuchadnezzar made an image of gold, whose height was sixty cubits and its breadth six cubits. He set it up on the plain of Dura, in the province of Babylon.

2 Then King Nebuchadnezzar sent to gather the satraps, the prefects, and the governors, the counselors, the treasurers, the justices, the magistrates, and all the officials of the provinces to come to the dedication of the image that King Nebuchadnezzar had set up.

3 Then the satraps, the prefects, and the governors, the counselors, the treasurers, the justices, the magistrates, and all the officials of the provinces gathered for the dedication of the image that King Nebuchadnezzar had set up. And they stood before the image that Nebuchadnezzar had set up.

4 And the herald proclaimed aloud, "You are commanded, O peoples, nations, and languages,

5 that when you hear the sound of the horn, pipe, lyre, trigon, harp, bagpipe, and every kind of music, you are to fall down and worship the golden image that King Nebuchadnezzar has set up.

6 And whoever does not fall down and worship shall immediately be cast into a burning fiery furnace."

7 Therefore, as soon as all the peoples heard the sound of the horn, pipe, lyre, trigon, harp, bagpipe, and every kind of music, all the peoples, nations, and languages fell down and worshiped the golden image that King Nebuchadnezzar had set up.

8 Therefore at that time certain Chaldeans came forward and maliciously accused the Jews.

9 They declared to King Nebuchadnezzar, "O king, live forever!

10 You, O king, have made a decree, that every man who hears the sound of the horn, pipe, lyre, trigon, harp, bagpipe, and every kind of music, shall fall down and worship the golden image.

APPENDIX: OBSERVATION SHEETS

11 And whoever does not fall down and worship shall be cast into a burning fiery furnace.

12 There are certain Jews whom you have appointed over the affairs of the province of Babylon: Shadrach, Meshach, and Abednego. These men, O king, pay no attention to you; they do not serve your gods or worship the golden image that you have set up."

13 Then Nebuchadnezzar in furious rage commanded that Shadrach, Meshach, and Abednego be brought. So they brought these men before the king.

14 Nebuchadnezzar answered and said to them, "Is it true, O Shadrach, Meshach, and Abednego, that you do not serve my gods or worship the golden image that I have set up?

15 Now if you are ready when you hear the sound of the horn, pipe, lyre, trigon, harp, bagpipe, and every kind of music, to fall down and worship the image that I have made, well and good. But if you do not worship, you shall immediately be cast into a burning fiery furnace. And who is the god who will deliver you out of my hands?"

16 Shadrach, Meshach, and Abednego answered and said to the king, "O Nebuchadnezzar, we have no need to answer you in this matter.

17 If this be so, our God whom we serve is able to deliver us from the burning fiery furnace, and he will deliver us out of your hand, O king.

18 But if not, be it known to you, O king, that we will not serve your gods or worship the golden image that you have set up."

19 Then Nebuchadnezzar was filled with fury, and the expression of his face was changed against Shadrach, Meshach, and Abednego. He ordered the furnace heated seven times more than it was usually heated.

20 And he ordered some of the mighty men of his army to bind Shadrach, Meshach, and Abednego, and to cast them into the burning fiery furnace.

21 Then these men were bound in their cloaks, their tunics, their hats, and their other garments, and they were thrown into the burning fiery furnace.

22 Because the king's order was urgent and the furnace overheated, the flame of

the fire killed those men who took up Shadrach, Meshach, and Abednego.

23 And these three men, Shadrach, Meshach, and Abednego, fell bound into the burning fiery furnace.

24 Then King Nebuchadnezzar was astonished and rose up in haste. He declared to his counselors, "Did we not cast three men bound into the fire?" They answered and said to the king, "True, O king."

25 He answered and said, "But I see four men unbound, walking in the midst of the fire, and they are not hurt; and the appearance of the fourth is like a son of the gods."

26 Then Nebuchadnezzar came near to the door of the burning fiery furnace; he declared, "Shadrach, Meshach, and Abednego, servants of the Most High God, come out, and come here!" Then Shadrach, Meshach, and Abednego came out from the fire.

27 And the satraps, the prefects, the governors, and the king's counselors gathered together and saw that the fire had not had any power over the bodies of those men. The hair of their heads was not singed, their cloaks were not harmed, and no smell of fire had come upon them.

28 Nebuchadnezzar answered and said, "Blessed be the God of Shadrach, Meshach, and Abednego, who has sent his angel and delivered his servants, who trusted in him, and set aside the king's command, and yielded up their bodies rather than serve and worship any god except their own God.

29 Therefore I make a decree: Any people, nation, or language that speaks anything against the God of Shadrach, Meshach, and Abednego shall be torn limb from limb, and their houses laid in ruins, for there is no other god who is able to rescue in this way."

30 Then the king promoted Shadrach, Meshach, and Abednego in the province of Babylon.

APPENDIX: OBSERVATION SHEETS

OBSERVATION SHEET

James 4

1 What causes quarrels and what causes fights among you? Is it not this, that your passions are at war within you?
2 You desire and do not have, so you murder. You covet and cannot obtain, so you fight and quarrel. You do not have, because you do not ask.
3 You ask and do not receive, because you ask wrongly, to spend it on your passions.
4 You adulterous people! Do you not know that friendship with the world is enmity with God? Therefore whoever wishes to be a friend of the world makes himself an enemy of God.
5 Or do you suppose it is to no purpose that the Scripture says, "He yearns jealously over the spirit that he has made to dwell in us"?
6 But he gives more grace. Therefore it says, "God opposes the proud but gives grace to the humble."
7 Submit yourselves therefore to God. Resist the devil, and he will flee from you.
8 Draw near to God, and he will draw near to you. Cleanse your hands, you sinners, and purify your hearts, you double-minded.
9 Be wretched and mourn and weep. Let your laughter be turned to mourning and your joy to gloom.
10 Humble yourselves before the Lord, and he will exalt you.
11 Do not speak evil against one another, brothers. The one who speaks against a brother or judges his brother, speaks evil against the law and judges the law. But if you judge the law, you are not a doer of the law but a judge.
12 There is only one lawgiver and judge, he who is able to save and to destroy. But who are you to judge your neighbor?
13 Come now, you who say, "Today or tomorrow we will go into such and such a town and spend a year there and trade and make a profit"—
14 yet you do not know what tomorrow will bring. What is your life? For you are a mist that appears for a little time and then vanishes.
15 Instead you ought to say, "If the Lord wills, we will live and do this or that."

16 As it is, you boast in your arrogance. All such boasting is evil.
17 So whoever knows the right thing to do and fails to do it, for him it is sin.

APPENDIX: **PRAYER AT A GLANCE**

PRAYER AT A GLANCE

What have you learned about God/Jesus/ Holy Spirit?		
What have you learned about prayer?		
What have you learned about yourself?		

A Collection on Prayer, Volume One

Major Texts

Life Application

Personal Takeaways

Other Notes

THE PURPOSE OF PRAYER

LETTER TO THE READER

Congratulations on reaching the end of this study! You are on an incredible journey of growing in your relationship with the Father through prayer. Thank you for making the decision to consistently show up in pursuit of this worthy goal.

If prayer still feels challenging, confusing, or inconsistent, please know this is okay. We aren't meant to figure it all out in one study. Prayer is a lifelong practice.

We do hope, though, that you now have some tools and truths to lean on and come back to as you continue to seek your Father in prayer. We hope you have found some community through this process and know that you don't have to go it alone. Most importantly, we pray you have encountered the heart of the Father, who has been with you all along and will continue to be with you.

We invite you to continue this journey with Volume Two of our Collection on Prayer, *The Promises of Prayer,* to discover all the wondrous things promised to us when we pray. We are praying alongside you on your journey!

God's grace abounds for you. You are loved.

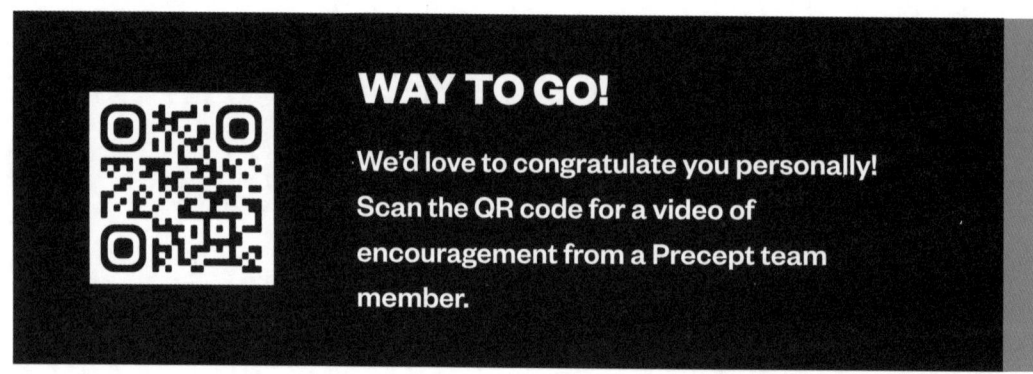

We hope you have enjoyed this Precept Bible study guide. We encourage you to continue your exploration of prayer by completing the rest of our Bible study guides from this collection!

The Purpose of Prayer
A Collection on Prayer, Volume One

The Promises of Prayer
A Collection on Prayer, Volume Two

The Power of Prayer
A Collection on Prayer, Volume Three

The Practice of Prayer
A Collection on Prayer, Volume Four